"Salmansohn is a powerhouse of a business woman, succeeding in a competitive industry by incorporating the many techniques she offers up in this book. Her insights are right on and universally valuable for people in all careers, and in all phases of their career."
—**KEITH KRACH,** founder and former CEO of Ariba

"This book is a must-read for anyone who wants to be more successful in business, or frankly, in life. There are many business books out there, but it is the unique style of Karen Salmansohn's book that makes these tips actionable, memorable and effective. I've ordered a copy for all of my sales staff... and my board of directors."
—**DOUG FIERRO,** president and CEO of WMI

"In a crowded field of new books, *Ballsy* is a standout: It's wise, witty and entertaining."
—**ANITA SHARPE,** co-founder of *Worthwhile* magazine

"The business world has never been more complicated. Salmansohn cuts through the clutter of advice and offers up an effective strategy for zooming to the top, with less stress and more fun."
—**ALAIN ROSTAIN,** president and founder of Creative Advantage, Inc.

"It takes balls to write, read and live this material. It truly distills good leadership to its essence with humor, insight and intelligence. Read it once, read it twice and give it as presents many more times."
—**JON STAENBERG,** venture capitalist and partner of Rustic Canyon Partners

"It's very simple. If you want to be happy and successful, read the book—be on the ball. If you want to live on the edge, wildly happy and successful—be on both balls, read the book twice."
—**PETER FRIEDMAN,** chairman and CEO of LiveWorld, Inc.

"Bold, innovative, wise, funny, straight-shooting, inspiring, and incredibly helpful techniques for fulfilling your dreams. *Ballsy* is a practical book that's fun to read. Laugh, smile, think, learn and then go succeed!"
—**ROBERT LEVITAN,** co-founder of iVillage and CEO of Pando Networks, Inc.

"Karen Salmansohn has done it again. *Ballsy* quantifies business chutzpah in a must-read, career-altering tome. Move over Jack Welsh, Karen's been unleashed."
—**GENE SEIDMAN,** managing director of Outhink, Inc.

BALLSY

HOW TO GROW A BIGGER PAIR
AND SCORE EXTREME BUSINESS SUCCESS

KAREN SALMANSOHN

HOW
books

An Imprint of F+W Publications

10 09 08 07 06   5 4 3 2 1

Distributed in Canada by Fraser Direct
100 Armstrong Avenue
Georgetown, ON, Canada L7G 5S4
Tel: (905) 877-4411

Distributed in the U.K. and Europe by David & Charles
Brunel House, Newton Abbot, Devon, TQ12 4PU, England
Tel: (+44) 1626 323200, Fax: (+44) 1626 323319
E-mail: mail@davidandcharles.co.uk

Distributed in Australia by Capricorn Link
P.O. Box 704, Windsor, NSW 2756 Australia
Tel: (02) 4577-3555

Library of Congress Cataloging-in-Publication Data
Salmansohn, Karen.
Ballsy : 99 ways to grow a bigger pair and score
extreme business success / by Karen Salmansohn.
p. cm.
ISBN-10: 1-58180-816-x
ISBN-13: 978-1-58180-816-2 (pbk. : alk. paper)
1. Career development. 2. Success in business. I. Title.
HF5381.S2557 2006
650.1--dc22
2005033070

TRUE FAILURE ONLY HAPPENS WHEN YOU ABANDON YOUR QUEST.

Keep on questing.

about the author

*ABOUT THE AUTHOR

Karen Salmansohn is a best-selling author and motivational speaker with twenty-eight published books, including *How to Be Happy, Dammit, The 8-Minute Guts Builder, The 7 Lively Sins,* and many others. She has worked on five TV development deals to create original sitcoms. Four of her books have been optioned: film options for *How to Make Your Man Behave in 21 Days or Less Using the Secrets of Professional Dog Trainers* and for her novel *50% Off*; and TV options for *How to Succeed in Business Without a Penis* and *Whip Your Career Into Submission.* She is a lifestyle expert on various TV shows and an ad agency veteran who still operates as a creative consultant for agencies and TV networks. She also gives motivational seminars nationally and internationally. For more information, visit www.notsalmon.com. For questions, comments, and to report ballsy stories, write Karen at info@notsalmon.com.

YOU CAN LISTEN TO KAREN ON YOUR
IPOD OR COMPUTER. CHECK OUT HER
DOWNLOADS AT WWW.IAMPLIFY.COM.

INTRODUCTION
introduction

In this über-competitive career marketplace, talent is only about 3% of the success pie. If you want to stand out and move forward, you must pay attention to that other, heftier, 97% part of your skill sets.

DON'T GET ME WRONG:

It's important to be good at what you do. Hell, to be fantastic at what you do.

But... even fantastic talent will only get you so far. Ultimate career success is based solely (and definitively) on **HOW WELL YOU WIELD YOUR 3% TALENT.**

HENCE:

This is why the tips in this book will aid anyone in any career—because they are "wielding" tips, not tips to improve your specific 3% talent. And all of these tips not only come from my own fall-down-skinned-knee-push-up-even-higher experience as an in-the-trenches best-selling author/book packager... **BUT** these tips were also gathered from a range of colleagues and mentors whom I wildly respect for their talent wielding skill sets.

Basically these are time-after-time-after-time-tested techniques

for achieving success, money, happiness, fulfillment and respect in the career choice of your dreams. to take control of your career and **FINALLY** snag the extreme business success you very much deserve.

IT IS POSSIBLE! YOU CAN ENJOY A CAREER THAT'S ABOUT BOTH LOVE AND MONEY—NO MATTER HOW WEARY OR FRUSTRATED YOU MAY PRESENTLY BE!

And this unique business book is not only speedy to read, but will speedily actualize what you—right now—might feel is an unachievable career pursuit!

So enough with the intro. Without further ado, here are the tips you must follow if you want

WISHING YOU BEST OF LUCK, BALLSINESS AND THEN SOME...

Karen Salmansohn

tips ^{no.}**1&2**

MORE IMPORTANT THAN TALENT, HAVE BALLS.

SURE, TALENT MATTERS. BUT IF YOU DON'T HAVE BALLS, YOUR TALENT WON'T MATTER — BECAUSE NOBODY WILL EVER FIND OUT ABOUT ALL YOUR SWELL TALENT.

FACT:
IF YOU'RE SEEKING EXTREME SUCCESS, YOU CANNOT BE AFRAID TO GO AGAINST THE CROWD, MAKE MISTAKES, LOOK DUMB.

FACT:
EVERY MEMBER OF THE FORTUNE 500 CLUB COULD EASILY BE ELIGIBLE FOR MEMBER-SHIP IN THE MISFORTUNE 500 CLUB. THEY JUST KNEW THAT WHEN/IF THEY FELL ON THEIR FACES, THEY'D USE THE LEVERAGE TO PUSH THEMSELVES UP HIGHER.

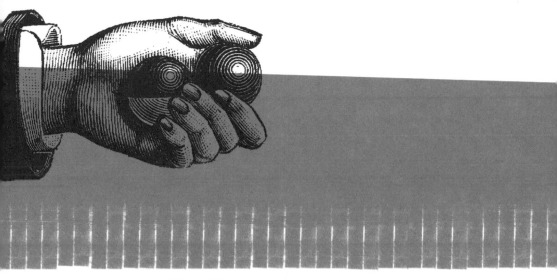

QUICK STORY:

A few summers ago I learned to windsurf, and interestingly enough, the first thing I learned was not how to windsurf! What my instructor, Bob, first taught me was **HOW TO FALL**. Bob showed me if I must land on my face, there's a safe way to land. Ditto for landing on my side and tush. Bob's goal was to remove my fear of falling so when I finally got up on the sailboard, I'd feel comfy about trying risky, fun, adventurous maneuvers! Well, this same metaphor applies—big time—to career life on land. You must become confident in your abilities to deal with any crisis or obstacle if you plan to pursue your passions with the cockiness, vigor and sense of playful adventure needed to snag 'em!

IN SUMMARY

IF YOU WANT TO REACH EXTREME HEIGHTS IN YOUR CAREER, GET OVER YOUR FEAR OF FALLING.

tip no.
3

THERE ARE NO WISHY-WASHY ROCK STARS, NO WISHY-WASHY ASTRONAUTS, NO WISHY-WASHY CEOS, NO WISHY-WASHY NOBEL PRIZE WINNERS.

Your success will always be only as large as your determination.

FOR THIS VERY REASON...

THE COCKROACH IS AN APT CORPORATE LOGO.
The cockroach has managed to survive everything nature and man has thrown at it for millions of years: volcanoes, floods, pesticides, radiation, predators... you name it.

You must keep this image of a cockroach in mind whenever you are out there selling your widgets to the world. No matter how many times you get sprayed with doubt, insults, sneaky competitors, slurs, sudden changes in the marketplace... after each and every seemingly lethal spray of negativity, you must quickly wipe off your antennae, find your bearings and keep going for all those goodies! Indeed, you must use each spray as a spirit strengthener to build up a stronger tolerance for dealing with future sprays of negativity... and thrive against all odds.

IN SUMMARY

Be like a *cockroach.*

REFUSE TO DIE.

tip no. 4

Mom was wrong.

It's okay to talk to strangers.

START FRIENDLY CONVERSATIONS OFTEN. SCHMOOZE. NETWORK. JOIN ORGANIZATIONS. GO TO PARTIES. GO TO GALAS. GO TO SOUP KITCHENS. NEVER HAVE COLD FEET ABOUT COLD-CALLING ANYONE YOU WANT TO MEET. DEPEND ON THE KINDNESS OF STRANGERS.

EVERY PERSON YOU TALK TO =
3 **DEGREES OF SEPARATION**
FROM SOMEONE YOU MIGHT WANT TO TALK TO.

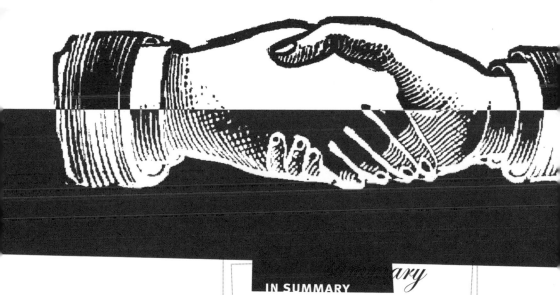

IN SUMMARY

THE MORE PEOPLE YOU KNOW,
THE LUCKIER YOU WILL BE.

tip ^{no.}5

Be immune to NO.

THERE IS ALWAYS A WAY IN
IF YOU ARE DETERMINED.

For example: **(1)** Listen to exactly where in the discussion that sound of "no" is emerging from. Often there's just a teeny tiny something stuck in between the "no" and the "yes." If you do a little buttering up... or give a small jiggle... that "no" sound can soon be gone without much work or change. **(2)** Listen to where the sound of "yes" is coming from... then give your client extra "yes" stuff and maybe he'll allow you your "no" as compensation for extra "yes"es. **(3)** Convince your client that you agree with her "yes" and that her "yes" is exactly the reason why you want to do

what she now sees as a "no"... because her "yes" actually backs up the reason for doing your "no." **(4)** Do your client's "yes." Build trust. Return later and re-present your "no." **(5)** If you asked on a Tuesday, return again on, say, Thursday or Friday. You might get a "yes" without ever having to butter up, jiggle or offer extra "yes" stuff. People are inconsistent. They randomly feel differently on random days. **(6)** Go forth and collect lots of "yes, yes, yes" from people the "no" person respects, fears or sucks up to. Make sure these "yes" people mention their "yes" to the "no" person. Return and collect your "yes."

IN SUMMARY

SUCCESSFUL PEOPLE ARE ADAPTABLE PEOPLE.
ADAPT A LITTLE AND THE WORLD WILL ADAPT WITH YOU.

tip no. **6**

IF AT FIRST YOU DON'T SUCCEED,
YOU'RE DOING SOMETHING STUPID.

Start blaming yourself more, others less…
and your career will surely rise.

Listen with an open mind to what the client and mar-ketplace are telling you about each and every failure.

DON'T JUST SEEK COMPLIMENTS. SEEK CRITICISM.

Consider each failure as a "full-ure"... full of lessons to improve your career.

Plus, even if you do succeed at a goal, study what you might have done better to exceed how you succeed.

IN SUMMARY

You must not only figure out what the client or market wants... you must also figure out what the client or mar-ket doesn't want... and then make sure you're not stupidly doing it/supplying it/saying it.

tip ^{no.}**7**

**PEOPLE AS A SPECIES ARE (1) FEARFUL.
(2) LAZY. YOU MUST (1) REASSURE CLIENTS
THAT YOUR WIDGET WORKS. (2) TAKE THE
"WORK" OUT OF A CLIENT'S WORK.**

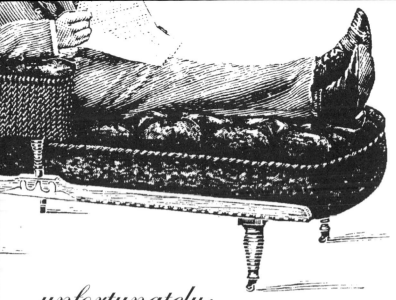

unfortunately:

You and I are also members of this same fearful and lazy species called "people." This means our first inclination might be to avoid doing extra work... or to not show extra specific details of our "widget vision" for fear of facing a very specific rejection.

but:

OFTEN THE ONLY WAY TO COMPENSATE FOR OTHERS' FEAR/LAZINESS IS BY SUPPLYING BOLDNESS OF VISION AND HARD WORK.

IN SUMMARY

Conquer people's natural instincts for fear and laziness by always being boldly specific about your "widget vision." Hold their hands as you hand work to them.

tip no. **8**

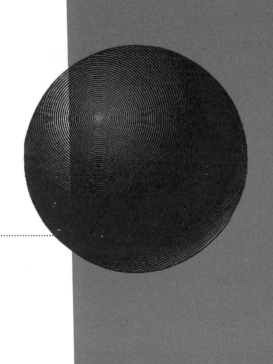

STOP GIVING 100%!

WHAT I MEAN BY THIS IS:
IN THIS ÜBER-COMPETITIVE CAREER
MARKETPLACE, IF YOU ONLY GIVE 100%,
YOU WILL ONLY GET AN OKAY CAREER.

IF YOU WANT A TRULY *fantastic* CAREER,
YOU GOTTA GIVE 150%.

YOU MUST ALWAYS GIVE MORE THAN WHAT
THE CLIENT/MARKETPLACE EXPECTS.

IN SUMMARY

BECOME KNOWN IN YOUR INDUSTRY
AS THE 150% PERSON!

tip no. **9**

Be intolerable.

What I mean by this:

ALTHOUGH BALLS ARE WAAAY MORE IMPORTANT THAN
TALENT, YOU MUST STILL BE INTOLERABLE ABOUT YOUR
TALENT. YOU MUST ALWAYS BE EXPLORING NEW WAYS TO
IMPROVE YOUR TALENT. EVEN IF/WHEN YOU EXPERIENCE
A SURGE OF MARKETPLACE LOVE FOR YOUR TALENT, YOU
MUST RESIST THE URGE TO COAST.

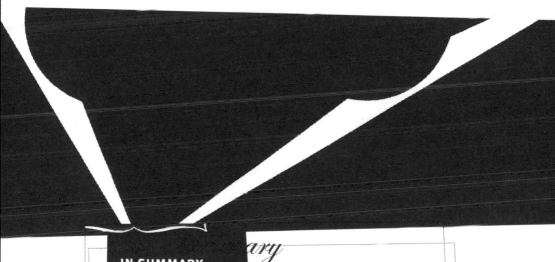

IN SUMMARY

USE YOUR 150% WORK ETHIC TO MAKE SURE YOU ARE ALWAYS PERFECTING YOUR TALENT.

tip **no.**
10

BE AN OPTIMIST

**FOCUS ON THE POSITIVE
RESULTS YOU SEEK, BUT
ALSO KNOW THAT THIS
UNIVERSE IS ONE OF**

Ebb and Flow.

WITH AN UMBRELLA.

IN SUMMARY

YOU MUST ALWAYS BE READY TO
EXERCISE YOUR EBB MUSCLES, SO
YOU'RE READY TO MOVE QUICKLY
OUT OF EBB AND BACK INTO FLOW.

tip no. **11**

FUN IS A HIGH-PERFORMANCE FUEL.

This universe has a bizarre sense of humor about when it decides to deliver its ebbs unto you. Usually they arrive at the most ironic moments (translation: most sadistic moments). It's up to you to make **FUN** your high-performance fuel to help you through these surprise ebb times.

(1) VIEW SURPRISE EBBS AS A FUN GAME SHOW — AND VIEW YOURSELF AS THE MASTER PROBLEM-MEISTER BEING TESTED TO FIGURE A WAY OUT OF THE EBBINESS.

(2) PRETEND THE CAMERAS ARE ON. LAUGH (HA HA HA), TELLING YOURSELF: "OKAY! VERY FUNNY, UNIVERSE! I GET IT! THIS IS THE PART, IN THE REALITY SHOW OF MY LIFE, WHERE THE SURPRISE TEST COMES IN TO CHALLENGE MY CREATIVE PROBLEM-SOLVING METTLE. NO PROBLEMO."

IN SUMMARY

VIEW PROBLEMS AS FUN GAMES TO DECODE, UNRAVEL, WIN. AND THEN GO OUT THERE AND WIN, DAMMIT!

tip ^{no}

PATIENCE IS *boring and unglamorous,*
BUT A HIGHLY NECESSARY VIRTUE.

YOU MIGHT NOT THINK ANYTHING IS CHANGING
IN YOUR CAREER, BUT IF YOU ARE PATIENTLY
PERSISTENT, YOU WILL SEE CHANGE.

CONSIDER THE DIARY OF CHRISTOPHER COLUMBUS:

MAY 4:
On this day we sailed on.

MAY 5:
On this day we sailed on.

MAY 6:
On this day we sailed on.

MAY 7:
On this day we sailed on.

MAY 8:
Discovered land. Ate corn.

IN SUMMARY

TRUE FAILURE ONLY HAPPENS WHEN YOU ABANDON YOUR QUEST. KEEP ON QUESTING.

tip no.
13
YOU GOTTA GIVE GOOD LUCK A NUDGE.

PREPARATION
+ (BALLS x 2)
= GOOD LUCK

Always have business cards on you, and if room allows in your briefcase, PR kits and samples of your widget. You never know who you will bump into and how they might benefit your career.

Once you have the preparation part of this formula in place, remember you **STILL** need the ballsiness to show off your goods and thereby experience the reward of good luck.

AS ANAÏS NIN ONCE SAID:
"One's life shrinks or expands according to one's courage."

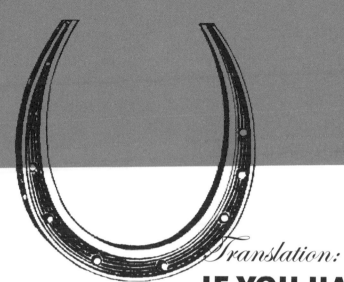

Translation:

IF YOU HAVE XL BALLS, YOU'LL EXPERIENCE XL SUCCESS.

IN SUMMARY

BELIEVE IN THE MIRACLE POWERS OF THE YOU-NEVER-KNOW FACTOR AND ALWAYS BE READY TO GO FOR IT... BECAUSE, HEY, YOU NEVER KNOW.

tip no. **14**

MAKE SURE PEOPLE HEAR YOUR TREE FALLING.

When something goes well in your career, call the right people and let them know. After all, a good career story heard has much more career momentum than a good career story never heard.

IN SUMMARY

WHEN A TREE FALLS, GRAB AS MANY PEACHES AS YOU CAN, AND GIVE THEM TO AS MANY PEOPLE AS YOU CAN.

tip no.
15

TO INCREASE YOUR APPEAL, NARROW YOUR POSITION.

Consider yourself toothpaste:

You must proudly know what is unique about your toothpaste and why it helps people more than any other toothpaste. You must ask yourself: What is my product tagline?

Use this tagline as often as possible in your phone calls, letters, conversations, packaging, web site, etc...

Summary

IN SUMMARY

DEVELOP A UNIQUE ONE-TO-THREE SENTENCE TAGLINE THAT IS WORDED IN A CONVINCING AND ATTENTION-GETTING MANNER... AND OWN IT AS YOURS AND YOURS ALONE.

tip no. **16**

LET PEOPLE KNOW WHAT'S IN YOU FOR *them.*

PEOPLE ARE NOT ONLY FEARFUL AND LAZY... BUT ALSO SELF-INTERESTED.

Think like a consumer or client to figure out how to create the tagline that will sell the toothpaste that is **YOU.**

During a sales pitch or meeting, shut up about yourself and listen very closely to hear what's most important to your consumer or client.

Listen for their unmet need. Listen for what might improve their lives. Listen for their biggest concerns. Then convince them that you/your widget totally fulfills their unmet need, will improve their lives, will delete their concerns.

Finally, rewrite their unique interests as your unique benefits in language that reeks of their self-interests.

DON'T SAY: WITH ME, YOU'LL GET 50% MORE BENZOARCHETAINE THAN OTHER TOOTHPASTES.

DO SAY: WITH ME, YOU'LL GET WHITER TEETH SO YOU'LL BE SEXIER, AND YOU'LL AVOID ALL THAT HORRIBLY PAINFUL DRILLING.

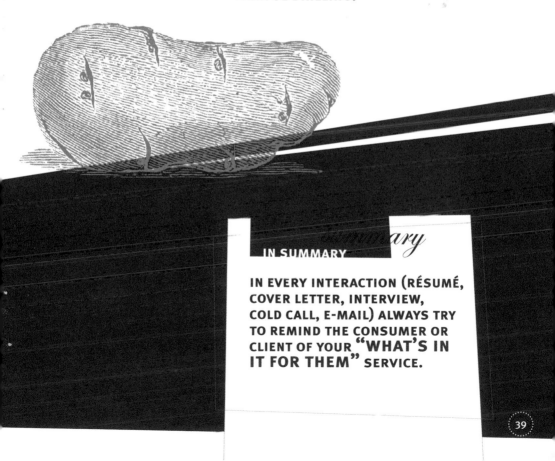

IN SUMMARY

IN EVERY INTERACTION (RÉSUMÉ, COVER LETTER, INTERVIEW, COLD CALL, E-MAIL) ALWAYS TRY TO REMIND THE CONSUMER OR CLIENT OF YOUR **"WHAT'S IN IT FOR THEM"** SERVICE.

Confiance garantie

tip no. **17**

DON'T WASTE PEOPLE'S TIME.

YOU'VE GOT BASICALLY TEN SECONDS TO SELL YOURSELF TO A NEW CLIENT WITH AN INTRODUCTION ON THE PHONE, WITH YOUR PACKAGING IN THE STORE, OR WITH YOUR WEB SITE PRESENCE.

Don't dial that phone or go to the printer or create that web page until you know your short, powerful, one-to-three sentence unique tagline pitch.

After you've announced yourself with your unique tagline pitch, keep the rest of your conversation and/or packaging copy short and to the point.

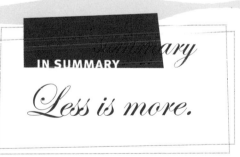

IN SUMMARY

Less is more.

tip no.
18

People hear what they see.

IT'S NOT JUST WHAT'S IN YOUR TOOTHPASTE BUT ALSO WHAT'S ON YOUR TOOTHPASTE TUBE.

Make sure you have appealing packaging:

**YOUR LOGO, YOUR ENVELOPES,
YOUR WARDROBE, YOUR SHOES, ETC.**

IN SUMMARY

Show well and sell well.

tip no.
19

ALL BUSINESSES BENEFIT FROM SHOW BUSINESS.

Make sure every presentation you give is dazzling, memorable and visually hypnotic, with lots of fanfare— or better yet, **FUN**-fare.

In today's attention deficit disorder world, you cannot merely memorize and recite, recite, recite. You must riff, rant, rave, wave, ad-lib, add humor and incite, incite, incite!

IN SUMMARY

IF YOU WANT TO BE CONSIDERED A BIG TICKET IN YOUR CAREER, MAKE YOUR PRESENTATION A BIG-TICKET EVENT.

tip ^{no.} **20**

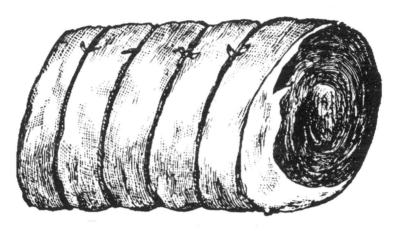

It doesn't matter how good your beef tenderloin is.
Don't try to sell it to a vegan store.

**WHEN LOOKING FOR THE RIGHT CLIENT/CONSUMER/
DISTRIBUTION MARKET/PROMOTIONAL VENUE...
ALWAYS NARROW THE FOCUS TO THOSE WHO "GET" YOU.**

DON'T GO LOOKING FOR LOVE IN ALL THE WRONG PLACES. YOU'LL WASTE TIME AND MONEY AND GET YOUR HEART BROKEN.

THERE ARE HERD IDEA PEOPLE.

THEN THERE ARE UNHEARD-OF-IDEA PEOPLE. ALWAYS TRY TO FIND AND WORK WITH THE UNHEARD-OF-IDEA PEOPLE.

THESE FOLKS WILL ALWAYS TAKE MORE RISKS AND GIVE YOU MORE FREEDOM TO FLEX YOUR TALENT. YOU'LL NOT ONLY MAKE MORE MONEY—YOU'LL HAVE MORE FUN MAKING YOUR MONEY.

IN SUMMARY

WHENEVER YOU WORK WITH
UNHEARD-OF-IDEA PEOPLE,
YOU'RE **ALWAYS** ASSURED
OF MERRILY SPEEDING AHEAD
OF THE STUBBORN, SLOWLY
GRAZING HERD.

tip ^{no.}**22**

WORK SMARTER HOURS, NOT LONGER HOURS.

SNIFF OUT THE BIGGEST BUCKS AND AIM YOURSELF IN THAT DIRECTION.

FOR EXAMPLE, IF YOU'RE A WRITER,
KEEP IN MIND THAT A MAGAZINE ARTICLE
QUICKLY BECOMES VAPOR.

BUT A BOOK CAN SELL FOREVER.
AND FOREVER MAKES A LOT MORE
MONEY THAN VAPOR.

IN SUMMARY

STAY DETERMINED NOT TO WASTE YOUR TIME
ON LESSER MONEY PROJECTS. AIM YOURSELF
MOSTLY WHERE THE BIGGEST BUCKS ARE.

tip ^no. **23**

EACH DAY TRY TO DO AT LEAST ONE THING THAT'S UNFAMILIAR OR SCARY.

FACT: YOU DON'T GROW UNLESS YOU STRETCH YOURSELF.
PROBLEM: Stretching yourself usually means you will feel (ugh) discomfort. You have to face your fear of the unknown and work on some new emotional and mental muscle groups.

FACT: MOST PEOPLE ARE...

(1) FEARFUL OF THE UNKNOWN

(2) COMFORTABLE WITH PUTTING IN THE LEAST EFFORT

(3) NOT WILLING TO PUT UP WITH SHORT-TERM PAIN FOR LONG-TERM GAIN

FACT: BUT NOT YOU, RIGHT?

IN SUMMARY

IF YOU WANT TO RISE UP HIGHER,
BE READY TO STRETCH HIGHER.

tip ^{no.}**24**

Get your unique *peanut butter* on the most desirable chocolate.

THE MOST DESIRABLE CHOCOLATE = PROVEN MONEYMAKING MARKET OPPORTUNITIES
UNIQUE PEANUT BUTTER = YOUR TALENT THAT UNIQUELY SATISFIES UNMET NEEDS
For example, I used to write feisty female books... until every girl and her grandmother started writing them. I then knew I needed to look for more highly desirable chocolate.

THAT'S WHEN I SAW UNMET NEEDS:
HIGHLY DESIRABLE CHOCOLATE = GAZILLION DOLLAR SELF-HELP BOOK INDUSTRY
I recognized that many folks still found self-help books embarrassing and time consuming. I figured if I could make them fun—short, hip and playful—I could snag extra sales. Plus I also saw a big potential for gift sales if the books looked snazzy. Then friends and family might be more likely to give self-help books as a gift... and feel safe that the recipient wouldn't slap them.

MY NEW KAREN-Y PEANUT BUTTER = MY EDGY DRY SENSE OF HUMOR AND GRAPHICS
How to Be Happy Dammit was born and became an instant bestseller.

IN SUMMARY

THERE'S A BIG DIFFERENCE BETWEEN A POPULAR IDEA AND A BIG-TIME-SELLING IDEA. THE MORE OUTSIDE THE BOX, THE MORE INSIDE THE PIGGY BANK.

tip ^{no.}**25**

BE A WEE BIT CRAZY.

Yes, I said crazy.

ALTHOUGH I DON'T KNOW WHAT BUSINESS YOU ARE IN,
A UNIVERSAL WIDGET MARKETING PRINCIPLE ABOUNDS:
IF YOUR WIDGET IS ONLY GOOD—AND NOT A WEE BIT
NUTTY—YOU'RE GONNA HAVE A HARD TIME STANDING
OUT AND MOVING FORWARD.

PAST CRAZY WIDGET IDEAS THAT MOST DEFINITELY STOOD OUT AND MOVED FORWARD:
FEDEX, STARBUCKS, CNN, CHRYSLER MINIVANS, POST-IT
NOTES, VCRS, FAX MACHINES, CELLULAR PHONES, HOME
COMPUTERS, JETBLUE AIRCRAFT, SEINFELD, JERRY SPRINGER,
BOTTLED WATER, THE INTERNET.

ary

IN SUMMARY

IN TODAY'S SENSORY-OVERLOADED,
ÜBER-COMPETITIVE WORLD, YOU'VE GOT
TO BE CRAZY NOT TO MAKE SURE YOUR
WIDGET/TALENT IS BORDERING ON CRAZY.

tip no.
26

THE WORLD IS CONSTANTLY CHANGING. *D*ON'T FORGET TO CHANGE WITH THE WORLD.

YOU MUST ALWAYS BE ASKING YOURSELF:
WHERE ARE PEOPLE BUYING WIDGETS THESE DAYS?
HAS DISTRIBUTION CHANGED? ARE THERE NEWER,
BETTER WIDGETS OUT THERE? HAVE MATERIALS OR
TECHNOLOGY CHANGED?

IN SUMMARY

YOUR WIDGET MIGHT BE GOOD... BUT
IN THIS SPEEDILY SHIFTING WORLD,
GOOD HAS AN EXPIRATION DATE.

KEEP MAKING SURE YOUR LADDER IS AGAINST THE RIGHT WALL.

Stay up-to-date not only on the outside world… but on the inside story of who you really are.

Have you changed in the last few years? Are you married? A parent? Divorced? Fatter? Fitter? Did you go through any life-altering changes? What interests you now? Who have you always been?

The more you get to know yourself, the more you get to know what makes you happy—and what your strengths and weaknesses are—so you can become the happiest, most successful YOU possible.

WITH THIS IN MIND... VOILA... SOME QUESTIONS ALL ABOUT YOU:

- HOW LONG DID IT TAKE YOU TO GET A CELL PHONE OR ON THE INTERNET? (HOW MUCH OF A PIONEER ARE YOU?)
- LOOK AT YOUR OLDEST ADDRESS BOOK. WHO ARE YOU NO LONGER FRIENDS WITH? WHY? WHAT CORE VALUES BROKE UP THESE FRIENDSHIPS? WHO ARE YOU HANGING OUT WITH TODAY VS. TEN YEARS AGO? WHY?
- WHAT DO YOU HAVE TO OFFER YOUR FRIENDS THAT OTHERS DON'T?
- WHAT DO YOU HAVE TO OFFER IN BUSINESS THAT OTHERS DON'T?
- ARE THEY SAME TRAITS? DIFFERENT?
- WHAT DO OTHERS HAVE TO OFFER IN FRIENDSHIP OR BUSINESS THAT YOU DON'T?

- AS A CHILD, WHAT WERE YOUR THOUGHTS ON SUCCESS AND MONEY?
- WHAT WERE YOUR PARENTS' THOUGHTS ON SUCCESS AND MONEY?
- HOW DID YOU MAKE THE FIRST DOLLAR YOU EVER EARNED? WHAT TRAIT LED TO ITS EARNING?
- WHAT WAS THE MOST AMOUNT OF MONEY YOU EVER MADE FOR YOUR TALENTS? WHAT TRAIT LED TO ITS EARNING?
- WHERE WERE YOU (IN MIND, PLACE, RELATIONSHIPS) WHEN YOU CREATED THIS HIGHEST MONEY-EARNING PROJECT?
- WHAT WAS THE WORK PROJECT YOU'VE BEEN THE PROUDEST OF? WHAT UNIQUE TRAIT OF YOURS LED TO ITS CREATION?
- WHERE WERE YOU (IN MIND, PLACE, RELATIONSHIPS) WHEN YOU CREATED THIS PROJECT OF HIGHEST PRIDE?
- WHAT IS YOUR HIGHEST AMBITION? IS IT MORE MONEY-ORIENTED OR PRIDE-ORIENTED?
- WHO DO YOU ADMIRE? WHY?
- WHO DO YOU RESENT? WHY?
- WHO DO YOU THINK IS THE HAPPIEST IN THEIR CAREER? WHY?
- WHO DO YOU THINK HAS THE MOST BALANCE IN THEIR CAREER AND PERSONAL LIFE? WHY?

- WHAT WAS THE FIRST MOMENT YOU KNEW CLEARLY THAT YOU WANTED TO PURSUE THE CAREER YOU ARE PRESENTLY IN? WHAT THOUGHT/INCIDENT/FEELING LED YOU TO BE ATTRACTED TO YOUR CAREER? DO YOU STILL FEEL THIS WAY TODAY— OR HAS THE CAREER HONEYMOON WANED? IF SO, WHY?
- WHAT IS YOUR BEST CREATIVE/PRODUCTIVE TIME OF DAY? WHY?
- WHAT ARE YOUR VULNERABLE NEGATIVE TRIGGERS THAT GET YOU SPINNING DOWNWARD?
- WHAT SELF-TALK DO YOU SAY TO YOURSELF WHEN YOU'RE COCKY?
- WHAT WOULD YOU DO IF YOU HAD UNLIMITED TIME... LIKE 1,000 YEARS TO LIVE?
- WHAT WOULD YOU DO IF YOU HAD LIMITED TIME... LIKE ONE YEAR LEFT TO LIVE?
- WHAT ARE YOU DOING WHEN YOU EXPERIENCE UNLIMITED METAPHYSICAL FLYING TIME... WHEN TEN HOURS FEEL LIKE ONE HOUR?
- WHAT WOULD YOU DO IF YOU HAD UNLIMITED MONEY?

IN SUMMARY

IT DOESN'T MATTER HOW FAST YOU GET THERE IF YOU'RE HEADING IN THE WRONG DIRECTION.

tip ^no. **28**

DON'T BE THE MICHAEL JORDAN OF BASEBALL.
BE THE MICHAEL JORDAN OF *basketball.*

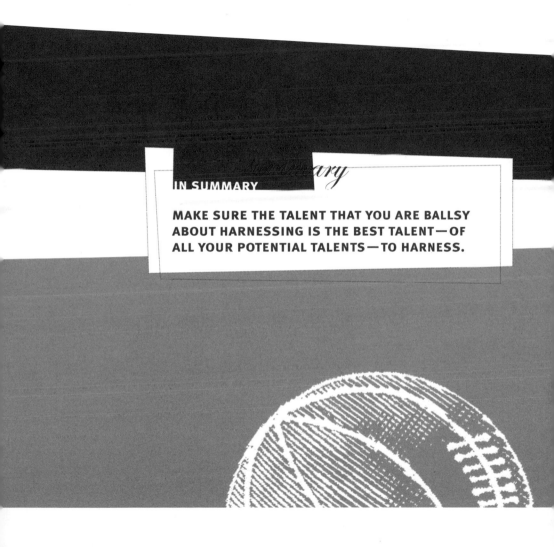

Summary

IN SUMMARY

MAKE SURE THE TALENT THAT YOU ARE BALLSY ABOUT HARNESSING IS THE BEST TALENT—OF ALL YOUR POTENTIAL TALENTS—TO HARNESS.

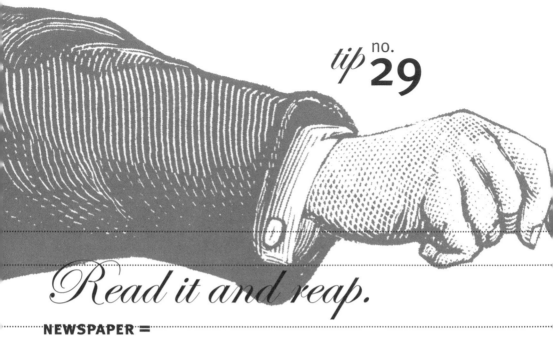

tip no. **29**

Read it and reap.

NEWSPAPER =
NEWINFORMATIONONHOWTOBEOFSERVICE

NEWSPAPER =
NEWCONTACTSHEET

NEWSPAPER =
NEWTRENDSTOCASHINON

NEWSPAPER =
NEWPRADASHOES

IN SUMMARY

**BE A "NOTICERADOMUS" OF
TRENDS AND ZEITGEISTS.**

tip no. **30**

BEND WITH THE TIMES

BEND WITH PEOPLE. BUT DON'T BEND YOUR STANDARDS AND ETHICS.

INTEGRITY MATTERS. LACK OF INTEGRITY WILL NOT ONLY TARNISH YOUR SOUL—BUT ALSO YOUR REPUTATION.

IN SUMMARY

Summary

**MAKE A DEAL WITH
YOURSELF. NO FOOTPRINTS
ON THE FACE. YOURS...
OR ANYONE ELSE'S.**

tip no. **31**

You're nobody until somebody hates you.

FOR EXAMPLE, MY BOOK **HOW TO MAKE YOUR MAN BEHAVE IN 21 DAYS OR LESS USING THE SECRETS OF PROFESSIONAL DOG TRAINERS** IS THE BOOK THAT PISSED PEOPLE OFF THE MOST... AS WELL AS SOLD THE MOST.

ACCEPT:

IF YOU PLAN TO BE A BIG SUCCESS,
THEN YOU PLAN TO MAKE WAVES.
ALSO KEEP IN MIND THE WORDS
OF PRESIDENT WOODROW WILSON:
"IF YOU WANT TO MAKE ENEMIES, TRY
TO CHANGE SOMETHING."

IN SUMMARY

YOU MUST NOT ONLY HAVE BALLS, YOU MUST HAVE
THE BALLS TO CONTINUE TO HAVE BALLS EVEN
WHEN PEOPLE TRY TO KICK YOU IN YOUR BALLS.

tip ^{no.}**32**

BE WILLING TO

You must accept that 99 out of 100 things you think up and blurt out might be plain silly (aka stupid)... but still you must be willing to think up and blurt out those 100 silly/stupid things so as to find that one brilliant thing that will make you filthy rich and fully fulfilled.

Also, never be afraid of embarrassing yourself by trying something you've never done.

To cure your fear of trying, merely switch your negative association of "fear" and "rejection" to "might make you filthy rich and fully fulfilled."

HUMILIATE YOURSELF.

IN SUMMARY

YOU HAVE TO BE WILLING TO ENTER NEW LADDER RUNG TERRITORY TO ENTER FILTHY RICH AND FULLY FULFILLED TERRITORY.

tip ^{no.}**33**

Think Grandiose Thoughts!

IT'S A FUNNY THING, *desire.* **OFTEN THE MORE EXCITED YOU CAN MAKE YOURSELF, THE MORE YOU CAN ACHIEVE.**

IN SUMMARY

DON'T AIM FOR A MERE PENTHOUSE. AIM FOR THE MOON.

tip no.
34

TIMING IS EVERYTHING—BUT THANKFULLY, PATIENCE CAN HELP YOU TO RE-CREATE BETTER TIMING.

EVEN THOUGH A BUSINESS CONTACT MIGHT NOT BE ABLE TO HELP YOU NOW, THERE'S ALWAYS THE POWER OF LATER.

SOMETIMES IT'S EVEN BETTER TO WAIT UNTIL LATER TO DO BUSINESS WITH CERTAIN PEOPLE. DON'T PREMATURELY SPEND YOUR DOING-BUSINESS COUPON.

ALSO, IT'S IMPORTANT TO HAVE THE FORESIGHT TO KEEP A COMPUTER WAREHOUSE OF YOUR PRE-ZEITGEIST IDEAS.

TODAY'S SILLY (AKA STUPID) IDEA CAN EASILY BECOME TOMORROW'S GENIUS IDEA.

IN SUMMARY

SOME IDEAS AND RELATIONSHIPS RIPEN WITH AGE... SOME MOLT. SNIFF OUT THE DIFFERENCE AND BE PATIENT ABOUT SERVING UP YOUR IDEA WHEN IT'S AT ITS PEAK... NOT PIQUED.

Familiarity breeds money.

Spread your word regularly. Lunch regularly. Send cute e-mails for no reason regularly.

OUT OF SIGHT =
OUT OF MIND =
OUT OF WORK

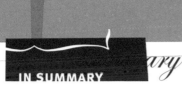

IF YOU ARE NOT SCHMOOZING REGULARLY, YOU WILL NOT REMAIN TOP OF MIND AND TOP IN YOUR CAREER.

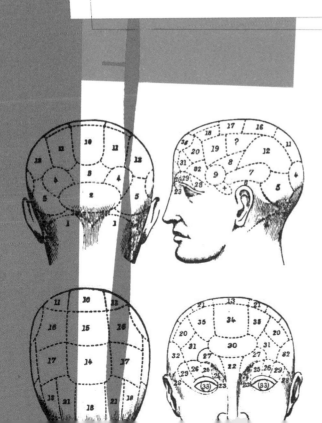

HUNT YOUR OWN HEAD

tip no. **36**

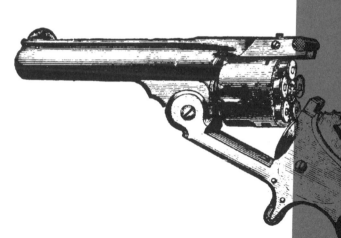

NEVER DEPEND SOLELY ON HEADHUNTERS OR AGENTS FOR WORK. NOBODY HAS AS MUCH SELF-INTEREST IN YOUR SUCCESS AS YOU.

IN SUMMARY

**IF YOU WANT TO
GET AHEAD, YOU MUST
ALWAYS SIMULTANEOUSLY
HUNT YOUR OWN.**

tip no.
37

PERCEIVED VALUE IS VALUE.

ASK FOR THE BIG BUCKS.
VALUE SHOULD NEVER BE YOUR POSITIONING.

YOUR UNIQUE SKILLSET SHOULD ALWAYS BE YOUR POSITIONING.

ALSO, BE AWARE OF THE DEADLY MIDDLE.
YOU COMMUNICATE: "HI, I'M AVERAGE."

Summary

IN SUMMARY

SETTING YOUR PRICE IS LIKE SETTING A SCREW. A LITTLE RESISTANCE IS GOOD... AND WILL MAKE SURE YOU DON'T GET TOTALLY SCREWED!

tip no. **38**

LONG-TERM GREED IS SOMETIMES SMARTER THAN SHORT-TERM GREED.

BE GENEROUS WITH PEOPLE YOU HIRE BECAUSE PEOPLE WHO FEEL APPRECIATED ARE PEOPLE WHO FEEL MOTIVATED TO WORK HARDER.

PLUS IT'S ALWAYS GOOD TO CUT AN OCCASIONAL DISCOUNT BREAK TO A LOYAL CLIENT OR A NEW CLIENT YOU'RE COURTING... SO YOU KEEP THEM LOYAL AND KEEP THEM HOOKED ON YOU.

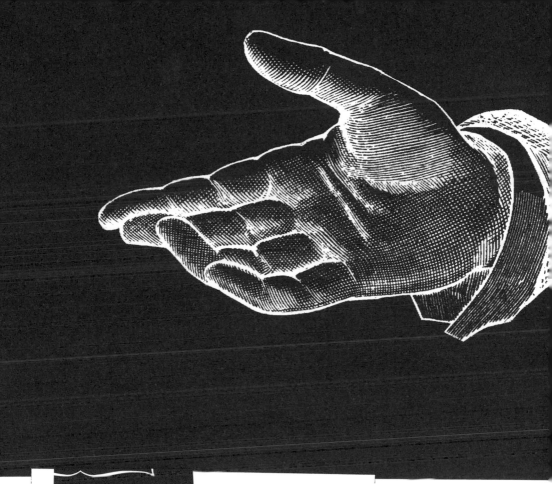

IN SUMMARY

SOMETIMES INSTEAD OF GOING FOR THAT ONE
MARSHMALLOW NOW, YOU SHOULD HOLD OUT
FOR THOSE THREE MARSHMALLOWS LATER.

tip ^{no.} **39**

WHENEVER POSSIBLE, PLAY WITH PEOPLE WHO ARE BETTER THAN YOU.

IN EVERY CAREER THERE IS ALWAYS A SUPERMODELER. GO GET CAFFEINATED WITH ONE. HEARING HER TALES OF GLORY WILL REIGNITE YOUR PASSION... AND MAYBE SHE'LL OFFER TIPS ON HOW TO BETTER WAG A TALE OR TWO YOURSELF.

IN SUMMARY

Summary

*Each month spend at least
some time with a Supermodeler.*

BE SOMEONE ELSE'S SUPERMODELER.

You learn when you teach.

IN SUMMARY

KNOWLEDGE, CREATIVITY AND POSITIVITY ARE CONTAGIOUS. GET INFECTED.

BE INFECTIOUS.

tip no.
41
PRACTICE THAT TONGUE TWISTER

THERE'S A BELIEF CALLED THE PARETER PRINCIPLE THAT 80% OF RESULTS COME FROM 20% OF ACTIVITIES.

MAKE SURE YOU DON'T GET STUCK DOING TOO MUCH IN YOUR 80% WASTE-OF-YOUR-PARTICULAR-TALENT'S-TIME PILE.

IN SUMMARY

KNOW THY LIMITATIONS.
WHENEVER POSSIBLE,
DELEGATE WHAT YOU SUCK AT.

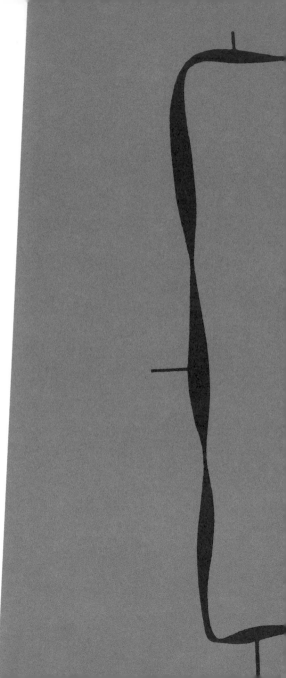

tip no.
42

CREATE
FUN
SHUI.

MAKE SURE YOUR WORKSPACE HAS LOTS OF BRIGHT LIGHTING...
PLAYFUL OR PLEASING DÉCOR...
PHOTOS OF THINGS THAT MAKE YOU SMILE...
AWARDS AND ACCOMPLISHMENTS TO MAKE YOU KVELL.

IN SUMMARY

GET TRIGGER-HAPPY.
SURROUND YOURSELF WITH THINGS THAT TRIGGER JOY.

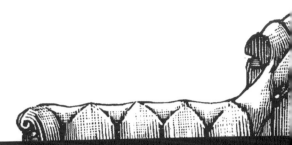

tip no. **43**

PRACTICE PSYCHE-OLOGY.

Convince yourself that you're psyched to work on your widget.

PASSION = DISCIPLINE

**WHEN YOU LOVE WHAT YOU DO, YOU DON'T MIND DOING IT,
AND SO YOU KEEP ON DOING IT... AND DOING IT.**

THE HÄAGEN-DAZS THEORY ON PRODUCTIVITY:

As you know, it doesn't take discipline to eat spoonful after spoonful of Häagen-Dazs. You can bet that nobody will ever say to you, "Wow, look at your discipline—how you just keep spooning down that pint!" Yet you keep on spooning. Why? You've got passion.

HOW TO GET YOURSELF PASSIONATELY SPOONING UP YOUR WORK:

(1) Remind yourself **WHY** you were passionate about your work in your honeymoon period... then ask yourself why your honeymoon waned. Un-wane the wane!

(2) Does your work improve people's lives? Remind yourself how what you do **MATTERS**!

(3) Ask yourself **WHO** you want to be, not just what you want to do. Get your identity re-synchronized as a successful, happy, confident, communicative, problem-solvin' genius of your craft, dammit!

(4) Link your success to something else... like baby needs a new pair of shoes... or mommy needs a new pair of Pradas.

IN SUMMARY

KEEP ON REMINDING YOURSELF WHAT YOU LOVE ABOUT YOUR WIDGET... AND WHY OTHERS' LIVES WILL BE IMPROVED BY YOUR WIDGET... SO YOU STAY IN A HEIGHTENED STATE OF EXCITEMENT AND PASSION TO WORK.

Hedonism
aids creativity.

HAPPY PEOPLE ARE MORE PRODUCTIVE—
AND EVEN RESEARCHED TO BE SMARTER.

THE FACTS:

Alice Isen, Ph.D, a professor in the psychology department of Cornell University's College of Arts and Sciences, discovered that radiologists who received a small present before work made more accurate diagnoses.

Yes, the gift literally increased the radiologists' mental gifts.

"Small inductions of positive emotion make people smarter, more productive and more accurate," says Dr. Isen.

So if you want to increase someone's performance in a task, be sure to supply a little goodie or a kind compliment before they do the task at hand.

And if nobody's around to dish out those small acts of kindness and tchotchkes of kindness to YOU, then go right ahead and self-dish. Treat yourself to a thought or thing that makes you happy, and then watch your performance and IQ rise!

IN SUMMARY

Bribe yourself to success.

tip no. **45**

EACH DAY, LEAVE PROJECTS AT A PLACE WHERE YOU'RE PSYCHED AND CONFIDENT.

YOU'LL BE MORE EXCITED TO RETURN THE NEXT DAY TO YOUR OFFICE AND START WORKING.

IN SUMMARY

WHEN YOU SEE YOUR WORKLOAD AS HALF
FULL OF CHAMPAGNE, YOU DON'T MIND
RETURNING TO FINISH THE OTHER HALF.

tip no.
46

BE A DILIGENT PROCRASTINATOR.

ALWAYS WORK ON MORE THAN ONE PROJECT AT A TIME... SO EVEN IF YOU ARE BORED OR FRUSTRATED WITH ONE... YOU ARE WORKING ON ANOTHER THAT HAS NOT YET BORED OR FRUSTRATED YOU.

summary

IN SUMMARY

DILIGENT PROCRASTINATION CAN MOVE YOU

QUICKLY FORWARD.

DON'T JUST CREATE DEADLINES.
CREATE ILL-LINES AND FUNERAL-LINES.

GIVE YOURSELF FAIR WARNING ABOUT DEAD-
LINES SO YOU'RE NOT SHOCKED TO SEE ONE,
AND TO ENSURE YOU ARE MORE SCARED—
IN A DAILY WAY—ABOUT ACHIEVING THEM.

ALSO, PLAN A SPECIAL EVENT TO EXPERIENCE
WHEN YOU FINALLY PUT YOUR DEADLINE TO
REST: A MASSAGE, A SHOPPING TRIP, ETC....

IN SUMMARY

**SCARE AND REWARD YOURSELF
TO REACH YOUR GOALS**

tip no.
48

DON'T JUST USE YOUR BRAIN, USE YOUR GUT.

Often your gut is smarter than that overthinking part of your brain—you know, that brain part that decides to take a thought apart so much it's hard to put the thought back together again.

Plus, your gut is also smarter than your underthinking brain—you know, that brain part that relies on focus groups (which often become de-focus groups).

YOU MUST NOT ALWAYS LOOK TO EXPERTS AND OTHERS FOR ANSWERS.

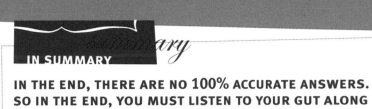

IN THE END, THERE ARE NO 100% ACCURATE ANSWERS.
SO IN THE END, YOU MUST LISTEN TO YOUR GUT ALONG
WITH YOUR OFT-TIMES GOOFY BRAIN.

DON'T JUST CREATE TO-DO LISTS. CREATE TO-UN-DO LISTS.

**JUST BECAUSE YOU'RE DOING A LOT,
IT DOESN'T REALLY MEAN YOU'RE DOING A LOT.**

**UNDO:
PERSONAL WACKINESS.
UNIMPORTANT MEETINGS.
UNCLEAR ASSIGNMENTS.
ENERGY-SAPPING PEOPLE.**

**MAINTAINING A CLUTTERED LIFE IS A GREAT TRICK TO
AVOID CHANGING YOUR LIFE.**

**GET A JOURNAL AND WRITE IN IT REGULARLY. LISTEN
TO YOUR INNER "TRUTH" ABOUT HOW YOU'RE WAST-
ING YOUR TIME WITH STUPID/FAKE/ENERGY-SAPPING
PEOPLE OR STUPID/FAKE/ENERGY-SAPPING ACTIVITIES.
THEN STOP WASTING YOUR TIME, DAMMIT.**

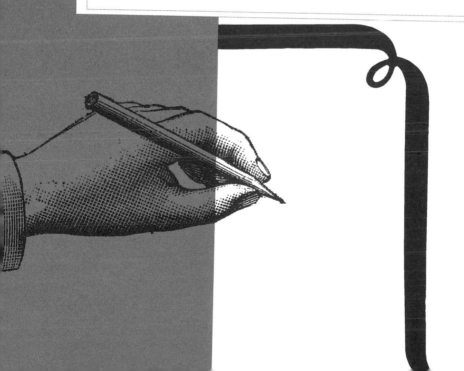

CAREER REMINDER:
TIME = MONEY. TIME WASTERS = MONEY WASTERS.

LIFE REMINDER:
JUST BECAUSE YOU SAVED THE TIME THAT MADE
YOU MONEY... SPENDING MONEY WON'T BRING YOU
HAPPINESS. ONLY SPENDING TIME WISELY WILL!

BOAST AND POST

tip no. 50

WRITE A LIST OF YOUR BEST
QUALITIES AND TALENTS.
POST THIS POSITIVE LIST IN PLACES YOU
CAN SEE DAILY. USE MEALTIMES TO SERVE
YOURSELF "THOUGHT FOR FOOD." RIGHT
BEFORE BREAKFAST, LUNCH AND DINNER,
NOURISH YOURSELF WITH YOUR LIST.

IN SUMMARY

**YOU THINK, THEREFORE
YOU ARE/AREN'T BALLSY.**

tip no. **51** LAUGH YOUR WAY TO THE BANK.

I've often joked that comedy is when bad things happen to anyone who is not me. Believe it or not, that's a Buddhist thought, because "anyone who is not me" = "the ability to separate one's ego from the situation and see outside yourself to how funny life can be."

You've got to try to lighten up about all those inevitable ebbs and ebb-bearing people.

AS NIETZSCHE SAID: "WHAT DOESN'T KILL YOU MAKES YOU STRONGER, GIVES YOU GOOD SCREENPLAY MATERIAL AND ALSO GIVES YOU A FUNNY ANECDOTE TO SHARE WITH FRIENDS OVER MARGARITAS."

(OR AT LEAST NIETZSCHE SAID SOMETHING LIKE THAT.)

THE POINT

Don't forget to enjoy the process of growing your career.

IT'S NOT THE FEAT. IT'S THE *emotion!*

It's not he who dies with the most toys who wins, but he who has the most fun playing with his toys who wins.

IN SUMMARY

ONE OF THE BEST WAYS TO ASSESS IF SOMEONE IS LEADING A TRULY SUCCESSFUL LIFE IS TO SEE HOW OFTEN HE LAUGHS WITHIN HIS DAY.

THE DOUBLE PUNCH-LINE SUMMARY THE HAPPIER YOU ARE, THE LESS STRESSFUL YOU'LL BE—AND THE MORE SUCCESSFUL YOU'LL BE.

SO LAUGH, DAMMIT, LAUGH!

tip no.
52

LEARN TO BE COMFORTABLE WITH UNCERTAINTY.

Uncertainty.

THE ONLY WAY TO RISE UP HIGHER IN YOUR
CAREER IS TO PURSUE SOMETHING NEW,
MORE, DIFFERENT—WHICH MEANS FACING
UNCERTAINTY!

AND IF YOU FEEL YOU ARE SATISFIED
TO STAY TREADING IN THE SAME PLACE
FOREVER—GUESS WHAT? THE CHANCES
OF THAT EVER HAPPENING ARE ALSO VERY

uncertain.

IN SUMMARY

YOU MUST DEVELOP A REGULAR DE-STRESS REGIME
TO DEAL WITH LIFE'S CERTAIN UNCERTAINTY.

CREATE A
SKILL-SET MUSCLE
FOR THE DAY

REGULARLY COME UP WITH A
SKILL-SET MUSCLE FOR THE DAY

For example, one day you might be "The Great Communicator" and really concentrate on how effectively you express your ideas to others. The next day, you might be "La Listener Extraordinaire," and decide to talk 30% less, listen 150% more.

OTHER SKILL-SET MUSCLES TO PRACTICE FLEXING:
The Problemeister Master, The Giant Wind of Change, The Positivity Orb, The Love Messenger, The Miracle Magnet.

WHY DOES THIS DAILY SKILL-SET MUSCLE MAGNIFICATION IMPROVE ONE'S CAREER?

We walk around thinking, "Hell, I should be so much more successful, loved, happy." But... are we really **TRULY** incorporating into our day the skill sets that are needed for all this? Sometimes we forget to be good listeners, stay positive, be loving. By focusing in on specific skill sets on different days, it's like focusing in on different muscle groups at the gym. You are ensuring you get around to all of the key skill sets needed to stay emotionally balanced and in good mental shape... so you can snag that happy, successful, fulfilling life that you so much deserve!

IN SUMMARY

EXERCISE A DIFFERENT SKILL SET EACH DAY, AND SOON YOU'LL BE PERFORMING AT YOUR HIGHEST LEVELS.

tip ^{no.}**54**

USE YOUR MORNINGS TO GET FIRED UP AND AIM YOURSELF LIKE A HUMAN CANNONBALL AT YOUR GOALS!

IF YOU DON'T HAVE A REGIMENTED MORNING PLAN, YOU WILL GO HAPHAZARDLY INTO YOUR DAY PELL-MELL.

AND...
PELL-MELL = CAREER HELL.

THEREFORE...
You must view your morning as the Decision Center for how to focus your day—and the earlier in the morning, the better.

Why?

(1) First thing in the morning, you haven't been beaten down yet, so you can still believe: "**BRAND NEW FRESH DAY = BRAND NEW FRESH START TO IMPROVE MY LIFE! WOOHOO!**"

(2) Your day hasn't yet started to **SWERVE OUT OF CONTROL,** forcing you into what's called "reactive state," reacting to life's demands as they bombard you. And reactivity is what messes up people's lives... leading people askew to get caught up with things that seem urgently important but are not **LONG-TERM-LIFE-IMPORTANT.**

(3) In the first hours of the morning, your head is still very clear and your spirit very cocky. You are in what's called "proactive state," where you can most proactively and wisely assign yourself **THE MOST IMPORTANT CAREER ACTIVITIES.**

IN SUMMARY

**USE YOUR A.M. TO AIM YOU...
AND THERE WILL BE NO STOPPING YOU!**

tip no. **55**

TRY THE CURE FOR NEGATIVITY...
ANTIDOTE THOUGHT THERAPY!

If your first thoughts of the morning are negative... do a little Antidote
Thought Therapy. For example, if you wake up thinking, "I suck. What if I
mess up this four o'clock meeting!?" write down Antidote Thoughts like, "I
was a star at that last meeting, I scored high on my SATs! I'm smart! I know
for a fact I have what it takes to make the client putty in my hands."

IMPORTANT:
Antidote Thoughts are very different—and much more powerful—than affirmations, because
they are **BASED IN BELIEVABLE FACTS** and therefore counteract your troublemaking subconscious. Basically, many of life's problems, conflicts and limitations—all that bad stuff that
pisses you off—are due to your troublemaking subconscious having negative, self-sabotaging
beliefs (most of which your conscious mind might not even know about). In contrast, affirmations don't dig deep enough into your subconscious because they're mere fluffy words, not a
convincing argument. SO... after you've written your morning Antidote Thoughts, you're now
ready to counteract any negative thoughts throughout the day about your upcoming four
o'clock meeting. If possible, try to narrow down your list of Antidote Thoughts into a single powerful word. In the case of being nervous about that big scary four o'clock meeting, keep telling
yourself: "Putty" or "Slam dunk." The more fun and playful the word, the more confident and
relaxed you'll be. Because you won't be taking yourself so seriously.

MAKE ANTIDOTE THOUGHT THERAPY A CONSISTENT MORNING HABIT, AND YOUR WORKDAYS WILL NOT ONLY BE LESS STRESSFUL, BUT A LOT MORE FUN!

tip ^{no.} **56**

DON'T JUST WAKE UP SMELLING THE COFFEE.
Go to sleep sipping the red wine.

IT'S NOT ONLY IMPORTANT TO USE YOUR MORNING
COFFEE TIME AS YOUR DECISION CENTER... BUT JUST AS
IMPORTANT TO USE YOUR EVENING GLASS OF WINE TO
VIEW YOUR DAY AS BEING AS HALF FULL AS POSSIBLE.

IN THE EVENINGS ALWAYS TAKE SOME TIME TO APPRECIATE
WHATEVER YOU DID TO MOVE YOUR CAREER FORWARD.

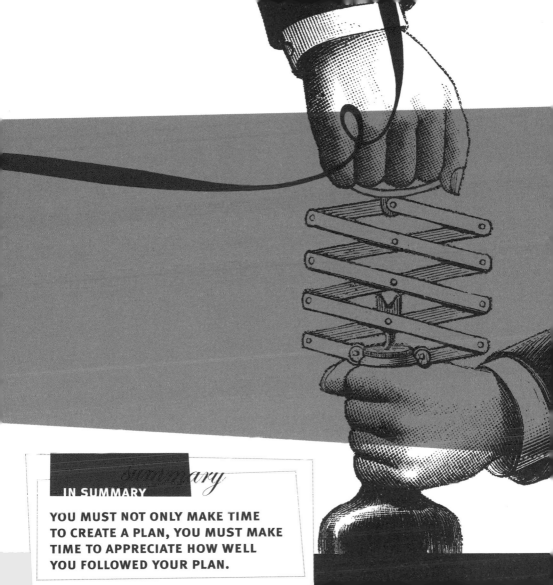

YOU MUST NOT ONLY MAKE TIME
TO CREATE A PLAN, YOU MUST MAKE
TIME TO APPRECIATE HOW WELL
YOU FOLLOWED YOUR PLAN.

tip no. 57

80% THINKING ABOUT THE SOLUTION.
20% THINKING ABOUT THE PROBLEM.

0% CHANCE OF A GREAT CAREER OTHERWISE.

BE THE MOST POSITIVE PERSON YOU KNOW.

tip no.58

A PACK OF PUPPIES LED BY A
PIT BULL WILL ALWAYS BE MORE
POWERFUL THAN A PACK OF
PIT BULLS LED BY A PUPPY.

IF YOU'RE THE LEADER, IT'S ESPECIALLY
IMPORTANT YOU LEAD BY BALLSY EXAMPLE.

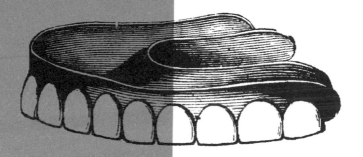

Summary

IN SUMMARY

A LEADER MUST MAKE
SURE THAT BOTH HER BARK
AND HER BITE ARE BIG.

tip no. **59**

KNOW THAT FAMILY MATTERS MATTER.

TRUE SUCCESS IS ABOUT
MAKING A LIFE...

NOT JUST A LIVING.

IN SUMMARY

YO! IT'S CALLED THE WEEKEND, NOT THE WEAKENED.

Relax.

Relax.

tip no.

EVEN A SCHMUCK CAN TEACH YOU THINGS.

DEFOCUS YOUR ANGER AT ENEMIES. REFOCUS THE LESSONS THEY GENEROUSLY TEACH YOU. IN THE END, YOU CAN LEARN JUST AS MUCH FROM YOUR TORMENTORS AS FROM YOUR MENTORS.

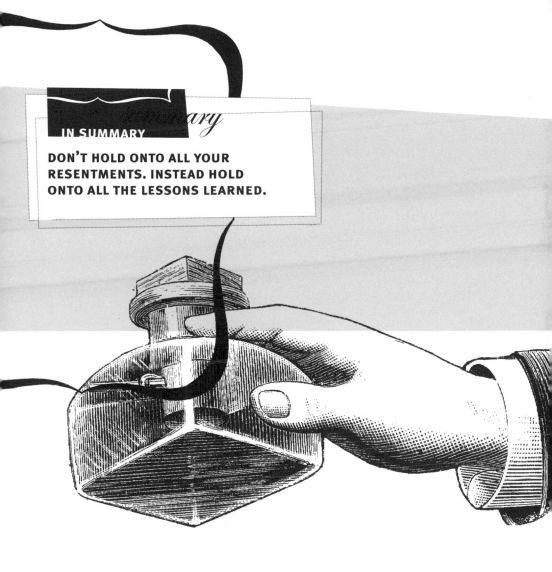

IN SUMMARY

DON'T HOLD ONTO ALL YOUR
RESENTMENTS. INSTEAD HOLD
ONTO ALL THE LESSONS LEARNED.

tip no. **61** # FIND THE ZONE.

STAY IN THE ZONE. DO AS MUCH AS YOU CAN WHEN IN THE ZONE.

THE ZONE IS THAT EUPHORIC PLACE YOU ENTER INTO WHEN YOUR WORK IS SMMMMOOOTHLY HUMMMMING ALONG.

HOW TO ZONE IN ON THE ZONE MORE OFTEN: LOOK BACK AND TRY TO FIGURE OUT WHAT YOU DID RIGHT BEFORE THE LAST TIME YOU ENTERED THE ZONE. WHAT LOCATION YOU WERE IN? WHAT WAS YOUR BODY POSTURE? WHAT WERE YOU THINKING ABOUT? WHAT WERE YOU WEARING? DUPLICATE AS MANY OF THESE THINGS AS POSSIBLE.

ALSO:

Lure your muse with music, give your brain a google, throw out old clothes, do a headstand and see the world upside down, write with your alternate hand, write with a crayon, move your desk, imagine what your twelve-year-old niece might say, do/see/eat something unfamiliar.

KEEP IN MIND:

Next time you find yourself naturally in The Zone, cash in on your neuron jackpot by doing as much as you possibly can. Tackle that difficult work project you've been avoiding. Make that uncomfortable call to a client. Leave yourself an excited message about how fantastic you are—a message that you can play back later to jumpstart that lost loving feeling.

IN SUMMARY

SUPPLE NEURONS = SUPER NEURONS

NEVER GET TOO COCKY. NEVER GET TOO BUMMED.

YOUR WORST TIMES IN BUSINESS:

(1) WHEN YOU GET TOO BIG FOR YOUR BRITCHES—
AND MAKE EGOMANIACAL DECISIONS.

(2) WHEN YOU'RE WORRIED YOU MIGHT HAVE
TO PAWN YOUR BRITCHES—AND MAKE
FEAR-BASED DECISIONS.

IN SUMMARY

ALWAYS WAIT TO MAKE IMPORTANT DECISIONS
DURING A BALANCED EMOTIONAL STATE.

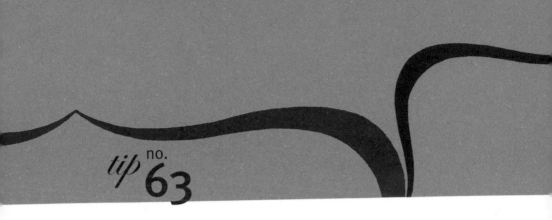

tip no.
63

WHATEVER BUSINESS YOU'RE IN, YOU'RE IN THE PEOPLE BUSINESS.

**IT'S NOT WHAT YOU KNOW—OR EVEN WHO YOU KNOW.
IT'S WHAT YOU KNOW ABOUT WHO YOU KNOW—
SO YOU CAN LET THEM KNOW YOU UNDERSTAND
THEIR NEEDS AND TRULY CARE!**

A Quickie Vocabulary Lesson:

**THE MORE YOU SAY WE! WE! WE!
THE MORE YOU HEAR OUI! OUI! OUI!**

IN SUMMARY

**THE BETTER YOUR UNDERSTANDING OF PEOPLE,
THE BETTER YOUR CAREER.**

tip no. **64**

BE A PLAYER.

**USE YOUR CAR'S CD PLAYER
TO TEACH YOU AND KEEP YOU
IN A PSYCHED STATE AS YOU
DRIVE TO WORK AND MEETINGS.**

summary

TIME = MONEY. TIME ENERGIZERS = MONEY ENERGIZERS!

tip no. **65**

Cold call at hot times.

IF YOU PURPOSEFULLY COLD CALL AT NIGHT, CHANCES ARE ASSISTANTS WILL BE HOME WATCHING TELEVISION WHILE THE BOSS IS STILL AT HIS OFFICE—AND ALONE TO PICK UP HIS OWN PHONE.

EARLY BIRDS ALSO OFTEN CATCH THE BOSS.

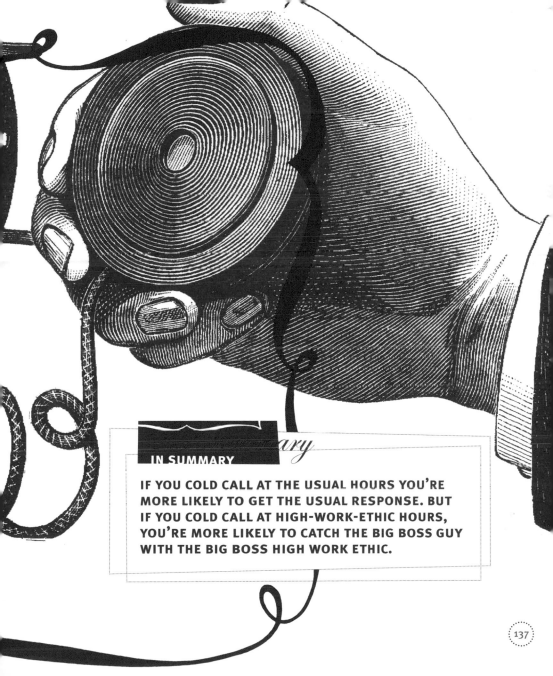

IN SUMMARY

IF YOU COLD CALL AT THE USUAL HOURS YOU'RE
MORE LIKELY TO GET THE USUAL RESPONSE. BUT
IF YOU COLD CALL AT HIGH-WORK-ETHIC HOURS,
YOU'RE MORE LIKELY TO CATCH THE BIG BOSS GUY
WITH THE BIG BOSS HIGH WORK ETHIC.

tip no. **66**

THE BEST THINGS IN A CONSUMER'S LIFE ARE FREE.

IF YOU BELIEVE IN YOUR WIDGET, YOU SHOULD FREELY OFFER IT FOR TRIAL—AND HOPE TO BAIT AND KEEP THE CONSUMER.

"FREE" IS THE MOST POWERFUL WORD IN A MARKETER'S VOCABULARY... FAR MORE POWERFUL THAN ANY MENTION OF A DISCOUNT OR CHEAPER PRICE.

IRONICALLY "BUY ONE GET ONE FREE!" WILL ALWAYS BE WAAAY MORE SEDUCTIVE THAN "50% OFF!"

IN SUMMARY

Summary

NADA SELLS A PRODUCT MORE THAN
A PRODUCT SOLD FOR NADA.

tip no. **67**

**RECOGNIZE THAT ALL ASSORTED
AND VARIED HUMANS ARE MOTIVATED
BY THE SAME EXACT THINGS.**

Yes, **YOU**—and everyone else on this planet—no matter how old you are,
how short you are, how smart you are, how attractive you are, what country
you're from, what sex you are—the whole human hoi polloi potpourri—
are all motivated by the same four motivations:

(**1**) DESIRE TO BE COOL

(**2**) DESIRE TO BE POPULAR

(**3**) DESIRE TO BE LOVED

(**4**) DESIRE TO BE UNDERSTOOD

ALL SUCCESSFUL WIDGET
MARKETERS EXPLOIT THESE
FOUR INTRINSICALLY
HUMAN MOTIVATIONS.

tip no.**68**

*B*UZZ MARKETING IS THE MOST POWERFUL BIZ MARKETING.

IN TODAY'S AD-SAVVY, AD-CYNICAL WORLD, CASUAL WORD OF MOUTH FROM FRIENDS AND STRANGERS IS MORE PERSUASIVE THAN GLIB WORDS FROM TV ACTORS—AND CAN BE MORE CHEAPLY BOUGHT THANKS TO BUZZ MARKETING AGENCIES.

A pssst about buzz:

Product placement—mentioning someone's web site (www. notsalmon.com) and a book title (*How to he Happy, Dammit*) in another book (*Ballsy*) that is highly appealing to your targeted audience—is also a highly effective marketing tool. Indeed, "branded marketing" is rapidly becoming a popular path for products, with marketers wrapping whole television shows around their product, rather than just slipping a commercial in.

IN SUMMARY

BUZZZZZZZZZZZZ YOUR MESSAGE TO FURTHER EXPAND YOUR BIZZZZZZZZZZZZZZZNESS.

tip ^{no.}**69**

KEEP CHANGING WHAT YOU KEEP CHANGING.

Sometimes you need to change your widget. Sometimes you need to change your distribution. Sometimes you need to simply slap on a new label.

ary

IN SUMMARY

MAKING NEW KINDS OF CHANGE WILL OFTEN MAKE NEW KINDS OF DOLLARS.

tip ^{no.}**70**

PRACTICE THE 4 REs CONSTANTLY.

RE-DEFINE.

RE-INVENT.

RE-STRUCTURE.

RE-ASSESS.

IN SUMMARY

RE-PEAT THESE FOUR REs AS OFTEN AS NECESSARY.

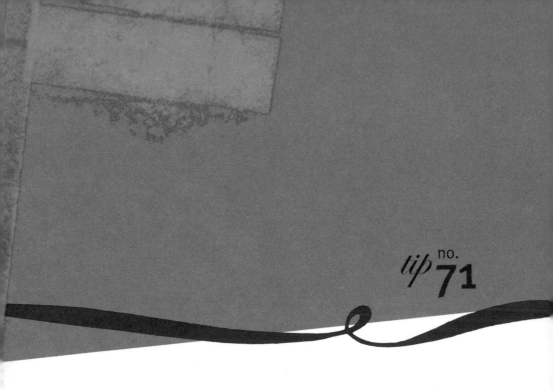

TALK IS NOT ONLY CHEAP — BUT CAN BE VERY EXPENSIVE.

ALWAYS GET IT ON PAPER.

HUG A LAWYER TODAY.
ONE OF THEM COULD SAVE YOU MONEY AND ANGST TOMORROW.

tip no. **72**

KNOW THY COMPETITION AS MUCH AS THY CUSTOMER.

MANY WIDGET MAKERS ARE MONO-SIMPLISTICALLY CUSTOMER-FOCUSED—AND THEREBY MISS OUT ON A BIG SECRET FOR HOW TO BEST PLEASE THE CUSTOMER.

Ironically, the best way to please your customer is by considering the competition.

Is the competition faster, stronger, better, juicier, more reliable, sexier, friendlier, snootier—and thereby just that wee bit more seductive to the customer?

What can you offer the customer that your competition cannot—and does your customer presently recognize your advantage?

summary

IN SUMMARY

BE AN ALERT SEDUCER—AND NEVER LET YOUR CUSTOMER BE SEDUCED AWAY FROM YOU BY THE COMPETITION.

tip no.
73

LEARN UNDER A "SUBSTITUTE TEACHER"

WHEN FACED WITH A PROBLEM, SUBSTITUTE SOMEONE YOU TRUST AND RESPECT AS BEING IN YOUR PLACE— AND IMAGINE WHAT THEY WOULD DO.

SOMETIMES SEEING THINGS FROM THE OUTSIDE CAN HELP YOU BETTER SEE INSIDE.

tip no.

LEARN NOT ONLY HOW TO READ SOMEONE LIKE A BOOK— BUT "SPEED READ" SOMEONE.

**SOME PEOPLE ARE SIMPLY NOT TO BE TRUSTED.
BUT FIGURING OUT WHO THEY ARE IS OFTEN NOT SO SIMPLE.**

BODY LANGUAGE EXPERTS SAY TO LOOK OUT FOR THE FOLLOWING:

(1) SCRATCHING ONE'S NOSE WHEN TALKING.

(2) LOOKING UPWARD AND RIGHTWARD DURING CONVERSATION.

(3) NOT LOOKING YOU STRAIGHT IN THE EYE.

(4) CONSTANTLY SAYING, "I'M GOING TO TELL YOU THE TRUTH HERE..." OR ASKING, "CAN I BE HONEST WITH YOU?"

(5) CROSSING ONE'S FINGERS BEHIND ONE'S BACK... NOT A GOOD SIGN!

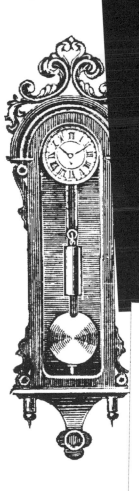

IN SUMMARY

YOU CAN TRUST SOME OF
THE PEOPLE SOME OF THE
TIME—SO MAKE SURE YOU
KNOW WHAT TIME IT IS!

tip no. **75**

EXPENSE REPORTS =
VULNERABILITY REPORTS

How do you spend your money? How do your colleagues
and clients spend their money? On vacations with a
spouse? Or on margaritas with underage hotties at the
local bar? How people spend their precious money re-
veals what they find most precious—and thereby offers
a clue into their psyches. You can use this information
to improve your own psyche, or to understand or speak
to another person's psyche.

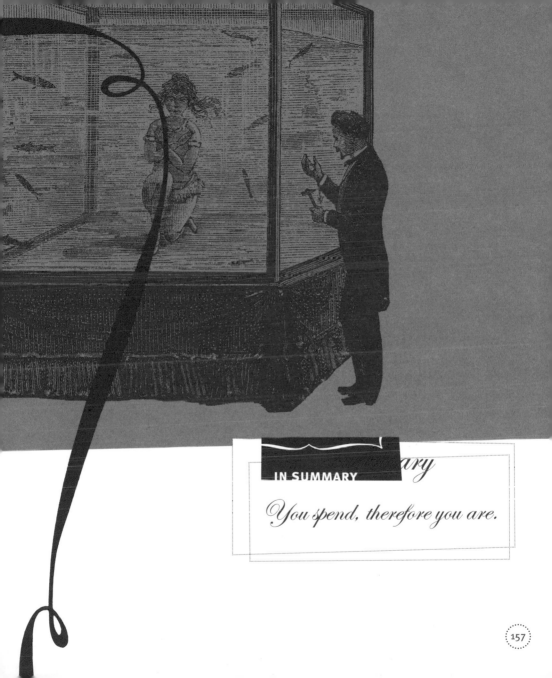

You spend, therefore you are.

tip ^{no.}**76**

ACKNOWLEDGE IS POWER.

After a job well done, take the time to appreciate your success.
Repeat the following mantra silently to yourself:

"DAMN I'M GOOD, DAMN I'M GOOD, DAMN I'M GOOD."
Put a star on your calendar on the date of this success so you can
later, at times of insecurity, recharge yourself with a reminder of
your "Damn I'm good" times.

DAMN, YOU'RE GOOD!

tip no. **77**

PUT YOUR FACE IN OTHER PEOPLE'S FACES.

When a big deal or big promotion happens, consider hiring an outside public relations person or calling up your trade magazine or newspapers yourself. Don't always wait for your company to do it.

IN SUMMARY

PR ABOUT SUCCESS BREEDS MORE SUCCESS.

**THE FIRST STEP TO STOPPING WORKAHOLISM
IS TO ACCEPT THAT YOU ARE A**

WORKAHOLIC.

**SERIOUSLY — THERE IS SUCH A THING AS WORKING WAAAY TOO HARD.
YOU NEED BALANCE TO CORRECTLY HANDLE HAVING THOSE BALLS.**

WORKAHOLISM OCCURS FOR MANY OF
THE SAME REASONS AS ANY ADDICTION.

Go to the Alcoholics Anonymous web site and look at the twelve steps
for recovery. Wherever you see the word "alcohol" replace it with the
word "work" — and then apply as many of the steps as you can to your
workaholism issues.

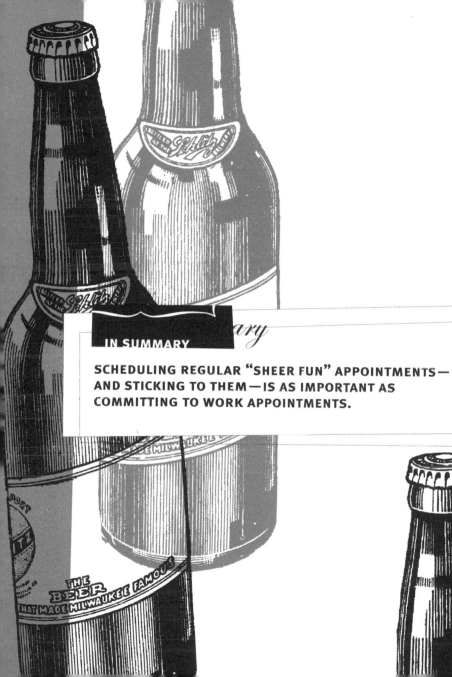

IN SUMMARY

SCHEDULING REGULAR "SHEER FUN" APPOINTMENTS—AND STICKING TO THEM—IS AS IMPORTANT AS COMMITTING TO WORK APPOINTMENTS.

IT'S BETTER TO GIVE THAN TO RECEIVE—

WHEN IT COMES TO PHONE CALLS.

The book *What They Don't Teach You at Harvard Business School* explains that you should always try to be the initiator of phone calls. It helps you stay focused on your work when you're working and avoid phone calls when you don't really need phone calls.

Also... if you do take an incoming call, always pause before picking up the receiver, and ask yourself what SINGLE goal you want to accomplish by conversation's end.

TRY TO KEEP ALL PHONE CALLS TO A TIDY
fifteen minutes or less.

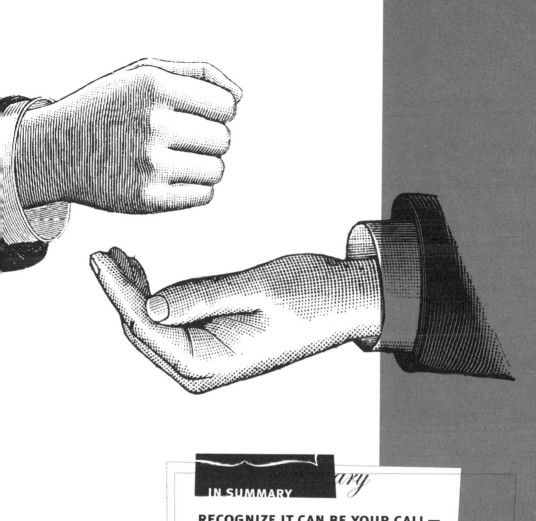

IN SUMMARY

**RECOGNIZE IT CAN BE YOUR CALL—
IF AND WHEN AND HOW LONG—
TO TAKE A CALL.**

tip ^{no.}**80**

Know your best damn hours to be your best damn self.

DETERMINE WHICH ARE YOUR MOST PRODUCTIVE HOURS FOR DOING THE HARDEST PART OF YOUR JOB. PURPOSEFULLY SAVE LESS IMPORTANT WORK TIME FOR DOWNTIME, NOT PRIME TIME.

KNOWING THYSELF CAN BOOST
THYSELF TO HIGHER PRODUCTIVITY.

tip no.
81

Play phone tag to win!

Notice what times specific people usually call you.
Voilà: A pattern will most likely form. Purposefully
call these specific people at these specific times.
Or ask people directly what times are best to talk.
Make planned-ahead phone appointments. Also, if
you want to motivate a game of phone tag to end,
leave a message to say if you don't hear back, you'll
assume no news is affirmative news.

IN SUMMARY

TOO MUCH PHONE TAG CREATES WORK LAG...
SO SNIP THOSE TAGS QUICK AND CLEAN.

tip no. **82**

Avoid red sweater / green sweater people.

AN OLD JOKE FOR MODERN TIMES:

A grandmother gives her grandson a red sweater and a green sweater for his birthday. Next time she sees him, he's wearing the red sweater. "What's the matter?" she asks, "You don't like the green sweater?"

IN SUMMARY

**RED SWEATER/GREEN SWEATER PEOPLE
CAN DRAIN YOU OF YOUR ENERGY—AND
ENERGY IS THE FUEL FOR SUCCESS.**

tip no. **83**

ℳAKE SURE YOU'RE HAVING ENOUGH "SKIN TIME."

SKIN TIME = CONVERSATION TIME, FACE-TO-FACE, NOT PHONE-TO-PHONE. BASICALLY, THE MEDIUM IS THE MESSAGE. IF YOU HAVE A LARGE MESSAGE TO DELIVER, YOU MUST NEVER DO IT ON THAT MEDIUM CALLED THE PHONE. IF YOU NEED CONFIDENTIAL INFORMATION, WINE 'EM AND DINE 'EM IN A RESTAURANT. IF YOU WANT FACTS AND FIGURES, CONFERENCE ROOMS ARE THE PLACE DE RÉSISTANCE.

IN SUMMARY

IT'S NOT JUST WHAT YOU SAY, IT'S WHERE YOU SAY IT.

tip no. **84**

IT'S NOT JUST REACH,
IT'S FREQUENCY—IN ALL MESSAGES.

**MAKING SURE YOU HAVE BOTH GOOD REACH AND
FREQUENCY IS A KNOWN TECHNIQUE IN ADVERTISING.**

**DITTO FOR ANY MESSAGE YOU HOPE TO
CONVEY TO COLLEAGUES, BOSSES AND CLIENTS.**

**FOR THE MOST PART, FREQUENCY EQUALS THREE
EXPOSURES OF THE MESSAGE FOR THE MESSAGE TO SINK IN.**

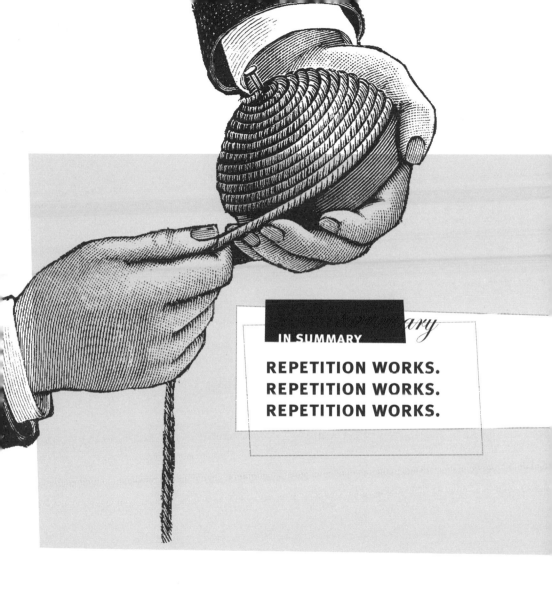

IN SUMMARY

REPETITION WORKS.
REPETITION WORKS.
REPETITION WORKS.

tip no. **85**

INDULGE IN
BRAIN FOOD
FOR THOUGHT.

SOME KNOWN FOODS THAT STIMULATE HIGHER THINKING:
Fish, meat, tofu, oranges, strawberries, wheat germ, broccoli, cheese, wheat grass juice.

SOME KNOWN VITAMINS THAT STIMULATE HIGHER THINKING:
Vitamin B, vitamin C, gingko biloba, ginseng, spirulina.

IN SUMMARY

YOU ARE WHAT YOU EAT—AND SWALLOW, IN VITAMIN FORM.

tip no.
86

ℰXERCISE YOUR DISCIPLINE MUSCLES TO EXERCISE REGULARLY.

THE MIND AND BODY ARE IN CAHOOTS.

If you want your career to be in good shape, you need to keep your body and health in good shape.

BIKE, HIKE, CYCLE, YOGA, RUN, SKIP, PLAY.

tip ^{no.}**87**

INDULGE IN REGULAR COCKYTALES.

READY TO GIVE UP?

Down a cockytale.

RECALL A TIME YOU BLEW A ROOM AWAY
WITH YOUR PRESENTATION OR IDEA.

MAKE YOURSELF SWAGGER.

THE SUCCESS STORIES YOU REMIND YOURSELF ABOUT CREATE SUCCESS STORY SEQUELS.

PRACTICE *tip* no. 88

ZEN ROCK

AND BOWL.

An old zen puzzle for modern times:

Pretend you have to fill a bowl with large rocks, pebbles, sand and water.
If you put the small things in first, it will overflow. The only way to fill the
bowl is to start with the largest rocks, then add the pebbles, then the sand,
then the water. Ditto with your business day.

IN SUMMARY

MAKE SURE YOU GET YOUR BIG
THINGS TAKEN CARE OF BEFORE
YOU USE UP TIME AND ENERGY
ON THE SMALL STUFF.

tip no. **89**

WAITING TIME CAN BECOME *Active Time.*

DECIDE NOW TO USE ANY WAITING TIME—FOR ELEVATORS, MOVIES, RESTAURANTS, RESTROOMS—EVEN CALL WAITING— AS TIME YOU WILL USE TO THINK A POSITIVE THOUGHT ABOUT YOUR CAREER.

TIME WAITS FOR NO ONE. BUT WHILE YOU'RE WAITING, YOU CAN USE TIME.

tip no. **90**

*I*T'S BETTER TO COMMUNICATE DIFFICULT STUFF SOONER THAN TO TRY TO FIX A REALLY DIFFICULT PROBLEM LATER.

**ALWAYS SQUOOSH A WORK PROBLEM WHEN IT'S A MINI.
THE LONGER YOU WAIT, THE BIGGER AND SCARIER PROBLEMS GET.**

CONFRONT WORK PROBLEMS AT THE SPEED OF LIFE.

tip no. **91**

KNOW HOW TO
RAISE A RAISE.

Before you go in for a raise, write up a list of all the ways you helped to raise money for the company. Did you help snag a big account? Increase profit margins? Always focus on your personal value—not your emotional reasons for needing a raise. Your boss doesn't care if your pet pit bull needs dental work—unless you can convince your boss that your pet pit bull can be trained to fetch lots of cash for the corporation.

Oh… and if you can't get the money you want right away, try to negotiate more vacation time or other perks.

**AND... ALWAYS LEAVE THE
BOSS'S OFFICE KNOWING:**

(1) IF YOU'VE SNAGGED THAT RAISE

**(2) WHAT IS NEEDED TO SNAG THAT
RAISE NEXT TIME**

IN SUMMARY

**SHOWING HOW YOU MAKE MORE MONEY FOR
YOUR COMPANY IS THE ONLY WAY TO GET YOU
MORE MONEY FROM YOUR COMPANY. DON'T
BOTHER TO MENTION YOUR PIT BULL.**

DON'T JUST TRUST YOUR FIRST INSTINCTS, BUT TRUST YOUR SECOND INSTINCTS. AND SOMETIMES EVEN YOUR 1,479TH INSTINCTS.

Think like Dr. Albert Szent-Gyorgy, the Nobel Prize-winning physician, who once said, "Discovery consists of looking at the same things as everyone else and thinking something different."

ACCEPT:
SOMETIMES IT TAKES A WHILE TO SEE SOMETHING DIFFERENT.

ACCEPT:
SOMETIMES DISTANCE CAN AID VISION.

ACCEPT:
SOMETIMES TRIAL AND ERROR CAN AID PERFORMANCE.

Be decisive—yet question everything.

IN SUMMARY

IF YOU KEEP GETTING TRIPLES AND NOT
HOME RUNS, CONSIDER RETHINKING YOUR
FIRST INSTINCTS FOR HOW TO SWING THAT BAT.

DANGLE, DANGLE, DANGLE.

WRITE DOWN YOUR TOP TEN MATERIAL GOALS FOR THIS YEAR, THE NEXT FIVE YEARS, THE NEXT TEN YEARS. FIGURE OUT HOW MUCH MOOLAH YOU NEED TO AFFORD YOUR DESIRES.

EVERY TIME YOU FEEL LAZY ABOUT PURSUING A WORK ASSIGNMENT, REREAD YOUR LIST TO INSPIRE YOU TO PERSPIRE MORE—AND THEREBY ACQUIRE MORE.

REREADING YOUR LIST OF GOALS CAN KEEP YOU FROM BECOMING LISTLESS.

tip no.
94

FEED YOUR MIND
WHEATIES FOR THE BRAIN.

You must condition your mind like an athlete conditions her body. A lot of fatigue comes from not disciplining your mind to resist negative thinking. Read self-help books to keep your mind at its most positive.

(Of course, in my positive thinking about what I write, I'd love to recommend some of my books. But, hey... I leave which books you read up to what you like to read. The important thing is that you just read 'em, dammit. Subliminal plug.)

Summary

IN SUMMARY

Eat your Wheaties.

**NOURISH YOUR CEREBRUM WITH A BALANCED
DIET OF POSITIVE, ENERGIZING THOUGHTS.**

tip no.
95

CHARITY BEGINS AT THE OFFICE.

EVERY YEAR MAKE SURE TO SET ASIDE AT LEAST 3% OF YOUR EARNINGS FOR YOUR FAVORITE CHARITY.

Summary

IN SUMMARY

Good karma begets good karma.

tip no. **96**

SHAKE IT
TO MAKE IT.

When you ask a question and want
a positive response, always shake
your head up and down—yes—as
you wait for the answer. It can work
as a subliminal reinforcer for that
yes.

yes

IN SUMMARY

THE SUBCONSCIOUS IS A VALUABLE BUSINESS ALLY.

SET MEASURABLE GOALS.

DON'T VAGUELY TELL YOURSELF:
MUST READ MORE.

SPECIFICALLY TELL YOURSELF:
MUST READ 3 NEWSPAPERS A DAY
OR MUST READ 30 MINUTES A DAY.

THE GOAL OF MEASURABLE GOALS:
YOU CAN KEEP TRACK OF YOUR FORWARD
PROGRESS.

WITH MEASURABLE GOALS, YOU CAN'T LIE TO YOURSELF ABOUT YOUR CAREER PROGRESS.

tip ^{no.}**98**

OFTEN IT'S EASIER TO CONVINCE YOURSELF TO BE GOOD FOR 15 MINUTES THAN TO BE A SAINT FOR A WHOLE DAY. SO, GIVE YOURSELF TINY "MUST-DO-TODAY-FOR-A-MERE-15-MINUTES" CAREER CHALLENGES.

MAYBE IT'S EXERCISING. MAYBE IT'S MAKING COLD CALLS. MAYBE IT'S KEEPING PAPERS MORE ORGANIZED.

WHATEVER.

YOU CAN ALWAYS FIND A MERE FIFTEEN MINUTES IN YOUR DAY TO DO THIS CAREER-BOOSTING ACTIVITY.
Interestingly, there's a Japanese word, *kaizen*, that means "small changes over time that add up to large changes over time."

Meaning, if you give yourself tiny fifteen-minute challenges, you will absolutely see a huge improvement in your career over time.

WHICH REMINDS ME OF A GOOD WOODY ALLEN JOKE:
Woody believes there is life on other planets and it is far more advanced than us technologically. Not because they are light years ahead of us... but because they are fifteen minutes ahead of us. If we all just had that extra fifteen minutes in a day, we could accomplish soooo much more.

summary

REGULARLY PICK ONE SMALL MEASURABLE CAREER CHALLENGE TO DO... AND DO IT.

tip no. **99**

COULDA
WOULDA
SHOULDA
Shuttuppa!

STOP BLAMING YOUR PAST FOR ANY PROBLEMS WITH YOUR LIFE AND START BLAMING YOUR PRESENT.

WHAT ARE YOU DOING RIGHT NOW TO HAVE THE LIFE YOU WANT NOW?

DECIDE RIGHT NOW TO DO SOMETHING RIGHT NOW WHILE YOU'RE STILL PSYCHED FROM READING THIS BOOK.

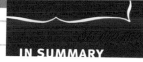

IN SUMMARY

PICK A MEASURABLE TASK RIGHT NOW THAT WILL GET YOUR NEW KIND OF PEANUT BUTTER ON THE DESIRABLE CHOCOLATE THAT ONLY YOUR TOOTHPASTE CAN OFFER... THEN GO FIND AN UNHEARD-OF-IDEA PERSON TO AIM YOURSELF AT...

...AND REFUSE TO DIE!

OTHER BOOKS BY KAREN SALMANSOHN:

ENOUGH, DAMMIT:
THE CYNIC'S GUIDE TO FINALLY GETTING EVERYTHING YOU WANT OUT OF LIFE

GOOD KARMA IN A BOX

HAPPINESS IN A BOX:
52 INSTANT MOOD BOOSTERS

HOT MAMA:
HOW TO HAVE A BABE AND BE A BABE

HOW TO BE HAPPY, DAMMIT:
THE CYNIC'S GUIDE TO SPIRITUAL HAPPINESS

HOW TO CHANGE YOUR ENTIRE LIFE BY DOING ABSOLUTELY NOTHING:
10 DO-NOTHING RELAXATION EXERCISES TO CALM YOU DOWN QUICKLY SO
YOU CAN SPEED FORWARD FASTER

HOW TO SUCCEED IN BUSINESS WITHOUT A PENIS:
SECRETS AND STRATEGIES FOR THE WORKING WOMAN

THE 30-DAY PLAN TO WHIP YOUR CAREER INTO SUBMISSION:
TRANSFORM YOURSELF FROM JOB SLAVE TO MASTER OF YOUR DESTINY
IN JUST ONE MONTH

THE 7 LIVELY SINS:
HOW TO ENJOY YOUR LIFE, DAMMIT

THE 8-MINUTE GUTS BUILDER:
A PORTABLE COACH TO PUMP UP YOUR COURAGE

THE BURN YOUR ANGER BOOK:
FILL IN YOUR IRE AND SET IT ON FIRE

MORE GREAT TITLES FROM
HOW BOOKS!

TOOTHPASTE FOR DINNER
HIPSTERS, HAMSTERS, AND OTHER PRESSING ISSUES

By Drew

This book is filled with wry observations, sarcastic musings, and edgy humor. *Toothpaste for Dinner* pokes fun at modern existence for 20- and 30-somethings, focusing on the things they think about—coffee, office cubicles, and hamsters.
ISBN 13: 978-1-58180-786-8, ISBN 1-58180-786-4, $9.99 paperback, 224 p, #33459

CREATIVE SPARKS
AN INDEX OF 150+ CONCEPTS, IMAGES AND EXERCISES TO IGNITE YOUR DESIGN INGENUITY

By Jim Krause

This playful collection of rock-solid advice and thought-provoking concepts, suggestions, and exercises is sure to stimulate the creative thinking that designers need to do their jobs well. Anyone working in marketing or design will find inspiration and new ideas with *Creative Sparks*.
ISBN 13: 978-1-58180-438-6, ISBN 1-58180-438-5, $24.99 hardcover, 312 p, #32635

INSPIRABILITY
40 TOP DESIGNERS SPEAK OUT ABOUT WHAT INSPIRES

By Pash

Written and compiled by Pash, this book offers an original take on one of the most requested topics by creative people—how to stay inspired when working on a deadline. Interviews with 40 of today's top designers and insights into day-to-day inspiration make this a must-have tool for everyone who needs a creative jolt.
ISBN 13: 978-1-58180-555-0, ISBN 1-58180-555-1, $34.99 hardcover, 240 p, #33011

SAVVY DESIGNER'S GUIDE TO SUCCESS

By Jeff Fisher

From marketing and promotion to client communication, this essential guide covers everything graphic designers need to know to achieve ultimate success. *The Savvy Designer's Guide to Success* is the go-to guide for creative professionals.
ISBN 13: 978-1-58180-480-5, ISBN 1-58180-480-6, $24.99 flexibound, 192 p, #32747